LIVING WATER

Devotions for Your Thirsty Soul

REV. GARY M. SCHIMMER

WESTBOW
PRESS®
A DIVISION OF THOMAS NELSON
& ZONDERVAN

WestBow Press books may be ordered through booksellers or by contacting:

WestBow Press
A Division of Thomas Nelson & Zondervan
1663 Liberty Drive
Bloomington, IN 47403
www.westbowpress.com
844-714-3454

ISBN: 978-1-6642-0156-9 (sc)
ISBN: 978-1-6642-0155-2 (e)

Print information available on the last page.

WestBow Press rev. date: 09/14/2020

Contents

Introduction

Living water is a metaphor spoken by Jesus to the Samaritan women at Jacob's well in the fourth chapter of the Gospel of St. John. This living water Jesus offered to her was a promise of "a spring of life gushing up to eternal life."

Scripture uses the metaphor of water to describe the new life that comes from God.

The Israelites were in exile. Their souls thirsted for a promise from God to rescue them and to set them free. So Isaiah prophesied, "Ho, everyone who thirsts, come to the waters." (Isaiah 55:1) Isaiah used the metaphor of water to give hope to the Israelites, refresh their souls, and remind them that God had not forsaken them. God provided the water of life.

In the cover of darkness one night, Jesus told Nicodemus, a leader of the Jews, about how one enters the kingdom of God: "Very truly, I tell you, no one can enter the kingdom of God without being born of water and Spirit." (John 3:5) For Christians, water and the Spirit is a reminder of Holy Baptism in which water is poured, God's promise is spoken, sins are forgiven, and one is welcomed into the body of Christ.

Visions from St. John the Divine provide hope in the midst of suffering and persecution in the book of Revelation. He wrote about Jesus, the Lamb, who promised the water of life to all believers: "for the Lamb at the center of the throne will be their shepherd, and he will guide them to springs of the water of life, and God will wipe away every tear from their eyes." (Revelation 7:17)

Our souls can become dry, and despair can set in. We find ourselves longing for spiritual refreshment. We long for the water of life to heal our souls and give us peace. The psalmist wrote, "As a deer longs for flowing streams, so my soul longs for you, O God. My soul thirsts for God, for the living God." (Psalm 42:1–2)

This book of devotions brings hope and spiritual refreshment for Christians and others seeking to draw closer to the presence of God. Each devotion in *Living Water* explores a theme using the following spiritual tools:

- Art image from a master artist
- Bible verse
- Faith story
- Quotation from Martin Luther
- Reflection questions
- Favorite hymn text
- Prayer

My purpose for *Living Water* is to enable you to grow in faith, encounter the living God, and reflect upon the goodness of the gift of living water from a loving Jesus Christ.

To God be the glory! The peace of the Lord be with you always.

Gary M. Schimmer
Pentecost 2020

The Baptism of the Eunuch by Rembrandt van Rijn, 1626

When Philip the Evangelist baptized the eunuch,
this new believer was marked with the grace of
God. He was marked with God's tattoo.

God's Tattoo

And the Lord put a mark on Cain, so that no one
who came upon him would kill him.

Genesis 4:15b

As I sat in the treatment room waiting for my infusion to treat the
cancer I was fighting, my eyes swept across the room to see those
who also sat in large, comfortable, gray recliners receiving their IV
cancer treatments.

A few of the patients looked weak and tired from the cancer that had
invaded their bodies and slept while others tried to pass the time by
reading or talking to another patient sitting beside them. I was one
of those patients who always brought a book to read as I sat for about
an hour receiving the medicine that slowly dripped into my veins to
stop the cancer's growth.

But on this particular day, I noticed the man sitting next to me. He
was an older gentleman with gray hair wearing a T-shirt and walking
shorts. His clothes really did not catch my attention, but it was what
was indelibly marked on his arms, legs, and neck that caught my eye.
Tattoos covered his exposed skin.

I looked at them as best as I could, trying to figure out what the
tattoos said and not wanting him to think I was staring at him. I did

not want to make him feel uncomfortable or lead him to think that he was an oddball.

I cannot remember all the tattoos marking his body, but one of them named a famous college and NFL football quarterback, Peyton Manning. After all, we were in Tennessee, and Peyton Manning had set passing records as he led the Tennessee Volunteers to many wins during his career.

After a few moments of glancing now and then at his tattoos, I mustered up enough courage to strike up a conversation with him. I wanted to know where he got his tattoos and why he had so many. I never got the answers to my questions, but we did make some small talk. I wished him well and mentioned that I liked his football tattoo. He seemed pleased that I inquired about it. With that, our brief conversation concluded. I then went back to reading my book, still wondering about his tattoos.

I will never forget that tattooed man marked from neck to ankle with names and symbols that were meaningful to him. But the encounter with the tattooed man led me to think in a spiritual way. It encouraged me to think about Cain, who was marked by God after he murdered his brother, Abel.

That mark from God was a sign to protect him from others who might want to harm him or even take his life. That mark on Cain was God's tattoo to make certain that even though he had done the unthinkable and slain his brother, God still had mercy upon him. God could still forgive him and give him a chance to repent and to move on in life.

In a spiritual way God also marks us. God leaves his divine tattoo on us in the sacrament of Holy Baptism. Forgiveness of sins, becoming his children, and making us his witnesses in this world is what God does for us in this sacrament. As water is poured on us in baptism and God's word is spoken, we are tattooed with God's grace. We are Christ's new creation.

In fact in the baptismal liturgy in Christian churches, the sign of the cross is marked on the forehead of the candidate for baptism. That mark is invisible, but it remains symbolically there forevermore as a reminder of God's mercy and grace for all the baptized.

In the New Testament, the apostle Paul wrote about baptism and how Christ marks us with his grace. In Galatians chapter three, Paul wrote about being clothed with Christ. This image calls to mind moments when parents and sponsors present the infant candidates for baptism at the font. Those infants are clothed in dazzling white gowns. Those white gowns are signs that the stain of sin is cleansed by Christ himself.

Meeting the tattooed man that day in the treatment room was much more than a moment to gaze at the tattoo markings on his body and wonder what they all meant to him. It was a kind of God moment when the Holy Spirit led me to reflect on how God marks us with his divine tattoo in Holy Baptism. So marked with the cross of Christ forever in this sacrament, we are free to live a life of faith and good works.

Quotation from Martin Luther

Baptism is an external sign or token. It separates us from all those not baptized so that we are known as a people of Christ, our commander, under whose banner (which is the holy cross) we continually fight against sin.

Reflection

Why is Holy Baptism important for you? What does it mean that in this sacrament we are marked with the cross of Christ forever? Think about whether this sacrament is significant for your daily life or if it's just a spiritual moment to recall in your past life. Do you think this quotation from Luther is an insightful way to understand the significance of Holy Baptism?

Hymn: "On My Heart Imprint Your Image"

On my heart imprint your image, blessed Jesus, king of grace,
that life's troubles nor its pleasures ever may your work erase.
Let the clear inscription be: Jesus, crucified for me,
is my life, my hope's foundation, all my glory and salvation!

Prayer

Lord Jesus Christ, in Holy Baptism you mark us from head to toe with your grace. Help us to ever be thankful for your precious gift. Amen.

Crossing of the Red Sea by Marten Pepijn, 1626

The Lord told Moses to stretch out his hand over the
sea so that the waters would drown the Egyptians.
This was the Lord's water rescue for the Israelites.

Water Rescue

So Moses stretched out his hand over the sea, and at dawn the sea returned to its normal depth. As the Egyptians fled before it, the Lord tossed the Egyptians into the sea. The waters returned and covered the chariots and the chariot drivers, the entire army of Pharaoh that had followed them into the sea; not one of them remained. But the Israelites walked on dry ground through the sea, the waters forming a wall for them on their right and on their left.

Exodus 14:27–29

I heard the shocking news about a rail accident on the radio one September morning in 1993. The Sunset Limited had crashed into the murky waters of Big Bayou Canot about ten miles outside of Mobile, Alabama, in the middle of the night when all was dark and still.

Minutes before that train attempted to cross the bridge over the bayou, an out-of-control barge struck the bridge support and weakened its structure. That unfortunate accident led to another accident of much larger proportion. In the rail tragedy, forty-seven passengers lost their lives in a matter of seconds despite their efforts to escape the waters that covered them and took away their final breaths.

The news report stated that uninjured survivors of that train wreck were taken to a rehabilitation hospital in Mobile to gather their thoughts and call loved ones. It just so happened that on occasion I was called upon to provide pastoral care on Sundays to the patients in that hospital. I did ministry there, so I took it upon myself to go there to assist the people who were struck with fear when the train crashed into the dark waters of that bayou.

When I arrived at the hospital, I encountered about thirty survivors who had gathered in a large room. Sharing their stories would be important for the survivors' emotional healing. Listening to them was one way I could demonstrate pastoral care and give the survivors moments to recall the details of the tragedy and express their emotions.

I remember talking to a young man, probably no more than twenty years old, who swam to safety. He had just visited his uncle, a Catholic priest, who served a parish in Mobile. Can you imagine the prayers for healing and strength rising up to God from that priest for the surviving passengers of the Sunset Limited? After all, his nephew and other passengers barely escaped death when their train cars plummeted into the dark water of the bayou.

Later in the week I read newspaper reports about the details of the train accident. Survivors said that when the train hit the water, they had only seconds to escape. They opened windows and doors as fast as they could to swim to safety on the shore. In the midst of panic and fear, the passengers had to think quickly about what to do to survive. In these moments, would passengers also think quickly enough to help other passengers make it safely to shore?

One young man from the Midwest repeatedly rescued survivor after survivor as he helped them swim to shore. Moreover, a mother and father helped their physically challenged child who sat in a wheelchair escape when water quickly filled their passenger car. They lifted their daughter up to the strong and waiting arms of rescuers to save her. But in doing so, they lost their lives. They sacrificed their lives so that their daughter could live. What deep and abiding love these parents had for their daughter even to giving their own lives!

Reflecting upon this tragedy, I became more aware of the fragility of life and the goodness of those who risked their lives to save others. That tragedy shocked me into thinking that I needed to make the most of every moment of my life. Life is precious. Life can be snuffed out through tragic accidents. I am to live with joy and thanksgiving because God daily bestows upon me an abundance of blessings.

The story of the Israelites crossing the Red Sea with Pharaoh and his army pursuing them comes to mind when I think about the crash of the Sunset Limited in the bayou outside of Mobile. Through Moses, God rescued his people. Moses stretched out his hand over the Red Sea, and it parted. A path of dry seabed opened up for the Israelites so they could hurry to safety.

But as Pharaoh and his army of chariots chased after them, the waters swiftly poured back into place. Pharaoh and his army could not escape. They would not survive. God had thrown horse and rider into the sea and rescued his people from Egyptian slavery. The water that poured in on all sides of the Pharaoh's chariots and army is reminiscent of what happened to the passengers of the Sunset Limited. No, the passengers were not being punished by God as they drowned in the bayou, but like the Egyptians who faced the power of walls of water all around, the passengers also faced water pouring into their train cars, giving them only seconds to escape to safety.

Scripture is brimming with references to water. In the beginning of creation before God spoke his word, there was darkness, chaos, wind, and waters. In the waters of the Red Sea, Pharaoh and his army were defeated, but God saved his chosen people. Jesus, God's Son, was baptized in the Jordan River, and God opened the heavens. God spoke and called Jesus his beloved Son. In Titus chapter three, we read that God saved us not because of anything we had done, but through the "water of rebirth and renewal by the Holy Spirit." (3:5) That water of rebirth is baptism, which saves from the threatening dangers of our sin. Our sins are drowned, and we are raised up to newness of life.

When the Sunset Limited crashed into Big Bayou Canot in the middle of the night, water was the chaos that took the lives of almost fifty passengers. Yet God saved over one hundred people in that train wreck as brave souls risked their lives for the sake of others.

Quotation from Martin Luther

For just as a child is drawn out of his mother's womb and is born and through this fleshly birth is a sinful person and a child of wrath (Ephesians 2:3), so one is drawn out of baptism and is born spiritually. Through this spiritual birth a person is a child of grace and a justified person. . . . Therefore sins are drowned in baptism and in place of sin, righteousness arises.

Reflection

Have you ever spoken to a person who has survived a natural disaster or a severe accident? What did that person say about how it changed their life? In the rail accident of the Sunset Limited, passengers were literally drawn out of the water to safety. Is the image of being drawn out of sin in Holy Baptism and connected to God's grace a good way to understand this mystery of faith?

Hymn: "Dearest Jesus, We Are Here"

Dearest Jesus, we are here, gladly your command obeying.
With this child we now draw near in response to your own saying
that to you it shall be given as a child and heir of heaven.

Your command is clear and plain, and we would obey it duly:
"You must all be born again, heart and life renewing truly,
born of water and the Spirit, and my kingdom thus inherit."

Therefore we have come to you, in our arms this infant bearing;
truly here your grace we view; may this child, your mercy sharing,
in your arms be shielded ever, yours on earth and yours forever.

Prayer

God of our salvation, we are your children through water and the
word in Holy Baptism. Give us strength and courage when the waves
of trouble surround us and save us from the danger of despair. Amen.

Pentecost by El Greco, c. 1600

When the promised Holy Spirit descended upon the apostles on the day of Pentecost, tongues of fire appeared on their heads. This fire from the Holy Spirit cast away doubt and fear and revived the apostles for a life of faith and confidence.

Revival Time

> All of them were filled with the Holy Spirit and
> began to speak in other languages, as the Spirit gave
> them ability.
>
> Acts 2:4

My Christian faith was developing when I was a child. My mother and I attended a Lutheran church while my father remained a Roman Catholic all of his life. The worship services in the Lutheran church we attended in the 1950s focused on the historic liturgy. Word and sacrament, hymns, and sermons and prayers were the main parts of the service.

Members of the congregation we attended were faithful, loving, and generous with their time, talent, and resources. They heartily sang the hymns and listened carefully to the preaching of the pastors. But there was never an outward display of emotion in the sense of clapping or shouting out a heartfelt "Amen."

So when a revivalist came to town, I was curious. The only thing I knew about revivalists and revivals was that participants outwardly displayed their emotions. In fact a revivalist and his crew set up a large circus-style tent on a vacant lot just a couple of blocks from my home next to the brick building of a major beer company. Would the revivalist who planted his tent in the midst of beer country preach against the evils of alcohol? Who knew? Nonetheless, the side of the revivalist's eighteen-wheel truck had the name of this church on wheels in big, bold red letters. As I recall, it read "David Epley Revival."

Within a day or two, the revival started. There was plenty of room on that vacant lot for people to park their cars. People came to this weeklong revival with expectations of being stirred up by the Holy Spirit for greater faith and witness. Still I wondered if some of them knew what to expect in terms of lively singing, stirring preaching, hand clapping, and altar calls. But on the other hand, there may have been some who were curious like me and just wanted to see and feel a different kind of religious experience.

It was the last night of the revival. I stood in the back of the tent and looked for the revivalist to start the service. There was something different about the revival on its last night. The musician was not playing the electronic organ as the people gathered and found their seats in those small wooden folding chairs. There was silence. No one said a word. It was dark. The lights in the tent were not turned on. That silence and darkness set the mood for a very somber service.

When all were seated and the stillness of the night had set in for the worshippers, the musician finally began to play a slow and soft tune. It was almost like a funeral dirge. One spotlight was finally turned on, and it gave light for all to see what was front and center. It was not a podium, nor was it an altar. It was a casket. Was this going to be a funeral service on the last night of the revival? One would think so.

All eyes were focused on that casket and all ears were attuned to the sweet and soft sounds of the organ music for a few moments. Suddenly, lights in the tent flashed on. The musician switched his music from soft and sweet to loud and lively. Then the highlight of the mood swing happened: the top of the casket flung open. Did the dead quickly and miraculously come to life? Who leaped out of that casket?

It was the revivalist himself who jumped out of that dark wooden box and began dancing around to the music. The people stood, caught up in the religious fervor, clapping and swaying to the beat of the music. I stood there staring at the outward display of emotion.

But there was even more to this moment of emotion and religious frenzy. The revivalists began to speak in a language I could not understand. Could the people who came to be stirred up by the music and preaching understand what the revivalist was shouting? I never knew. Later I learned that this unintelligible language was called glossolalia, or speaking in tongues. The Holy Spirit had so inspired and moved this revivalist to speak in a language only known to those to whom the Spirit gave knowledge to understand and interpret it.

I stood in amazement of it all. That was a far cry from the disciplined and historic worship I was accustomed to in the Lutheran church. On the last night of that revival, the Spirit worked mightily to stir up the hearts, minds, and voices of the people and preacher. The organist, filled with the Spirit, played the organ so loudly, as if he wanted the whole world to hear the sounds of his music.

I had never seen anything like it and had only heard that revival services were deeply and outwardly emotional. Perhaps that night I got a taste of the emotion that swept through our country in the eighteenth century's Great Awakening.

When the revival service ended, I walked home and sat on my front porch staring at the revival tent and trying to make sense of a much different worship experience. That kind of religious service was not for me, but it was truly one way the Holy Spirit called people to faith in the crucified and risen Lord Jesus Christ.

Quotation from Martin Luther

Therefore, we must concentrate on the term "Holy Spirit," because it is so precise that we can find no substitute for it. Many other kinds of spirits are mentioned in Scripture, such as human spirit, heavenly spirits, and the evil spirit. But God's Spirit is called a Holy Spirit, that is, the one who has made us holy and still makes us holy.

Reflection

Have you attended a revival? Think about your experience. What do you think Luther meant when he wrote that the Holy Spirit makes us holy? Can the Holy Spirit work faith in a person's heart in an emotional revival service as well as in a service using historic liturgy?

Hymn: "Come, Holy Ghost, God and Lord"

Come, Holy Ghost, God and Lord,
with all your graces now outpoured
on each believer's mind and heart;
your fervent love to them impart.
Lord, by the brightness of your light
in holy faith your church unite;
from ev'ry land and ev'ry tongue,
this to your praise, O Lord, our God, be sung:
Alleluia! Alleluia!

Come, holy Light, guide divine,
now cause the word of life to shine.
Teach us to know our God aright
as loving Father, our delight.
From ev'ry error keep us free;

let none but Christ our teacher be,
that we in living faith abide,
in him, our Lord, with all our might confide.
Alleluia! Alleluia!

Come, holy Fire, comfort true,
grant us the will your work to do
and in your service to abide;
let trials turn us not aside.
Lord, by your pow'r prepare each heart
and to our weakness strength impart,
that bravely here we may contend,
through life and death to you, our Lord, ascend.
Alleluia! Alleluia!

Prayer

Come, Holy Spirit, fill our hearts with love to share with people of every land and tongue. Give us the peace that the world cannot give and the joy that renews our faith and life. Amen.

The Last Supper by Hans Holbein the Younger, c. 1524–1525

When Jesus and his disciples celebrated the Passover meal, Jesus transformed it into a meal offering his own body and blood with the bread and wine. This Holy Communion is for you, me, and all believers in Christ.

My Communion

> While they were eating, Jesus took a loaf of bread, and after blessing it he broke it, gave it to the disciples, and said, "Take, eat; this is my body." Then he took a cup, and after giving thanks he gave it to them saying, "Drink from it, all of you; for this is my blood of the covenant, which is poured out for many for the forgiveness of sins."
>
> Matthew 26:26–28

As a parish pastor it was my practice to visit homebound members of the congregation and administer Holy Communion to them. Members of the Lutheran church believe that in this sacrament there is the real presence of Christ and his promise for forgiveness, life, and salvation. Neglecting the reception of this sacrament would leave people with a sense of hopelessness and despair. But with the body and blood of Christ, people find joy and thanksgiving because Christ draws close to them for abundant life.

As I served a congregation in Mobile, Alabama, my list of the homebound grew to be about twenty members. I was kept busy from month to month visiting them in their homes for holy conversations, prayer, Scripture reading, and giving the bread and wine of Holy Communion.

Some of the homebound members lived within a ten-minute drive from the church building while it took a half hour or more to drive to visit other homebound members who lived miles away. One of those members who lived over a half-hour drive from the church was a woman we'll call Helen. She lived in a nursing home in a small community called Citronelle about twenty miles outside of the city limits of Mobile.

My heart ached for Helen because her husband had died and left her with little money to live on. She depended on the women of the congregation to provide personal items for her and to visit as they had the time. Moreover, she had no family members who visited her. Her closest relatives in the Midwest sent her pictures of their family, which Helen displayed on a bulletin board in her room, but they never visited with her. Helen smiled and her eyes became big and bright whenever she talked about her family and shared those photos with me.

My visits and the visits of the congregation's women broke the loneliness in Helen's life. She was comforted by the fact that even though she lived in a small community, the church remembered her. She was part of the congregation, and her home's distance from the church would not sever her ties with the fellowship of believers who visited to show her Christ's love.

My visits to Helen always took a similar pattern. After we greeted each other, we always talked about her family and church life. But after those conversations, I would say to her, "Helen, would you like communion today?" Without fail Helen spoke the same words each time I offered her this sacrament: "I have to have my communion."

Yes, it was Helen's communion. It was a faith moment in which she claimed her relationship to Christ and his presence in her life. It was truly meaningful for her. It brought her hope and spiritual refreshment. As I gave her the wafer, I said, "The body of Christ given for you." In a similar manner I gave her the little cup of wine with the words, "The blood of Christ shed for you." Those words of promise from the Lord Jesus Christ assured Helen that her Savior drew close to her and would never forsake her. Christ's words, which we find in the gospels and which we hear each time the sacrament of Holy Communion is celebrated, reminded Helen of Christ's enduring love for her.

My monthly visit to Helen to give her Holy Communion was something she looked forward to and so did I. I bet that if I could have visited with her each week or even each day, she would always say to me, "I have to have my communion." I believe she would never tire of receiving Christ's gift of his own flesh and blood, his real presence, because Helen's faith was strong, and she yearned for those intimate moments with her Lord.

Quotation from Martin Luther

To receive this sacrament in bread and wine, then, is nothing else than to receive a sure sign of this fellowship and incorporation with Christ and all the saints.

Reflection

What does Luther mean when he describes Holy Communion as "a sure sign of fellowship and incorporation with Christ and all the saints?" When you commune, do you often think about your connection with saints (believers) of every time and every place?

Hymn: "I Received the Living God"

Refrain
I received the living God, and my heart is full of joy.
I received the living God, and my heart is full of joy.

Jesus said: I am the bread, kneaded long to give you life;
you who will partake of me need not ever fear to die.

Refrain

Jesus said: I am the way, and my Father longs for you;
so I come to bring you home to be one with us anew.

Refrain

Jesus said: I am the truth; come and follow close to me.
You will know me in your heart, and my word shall make you free.

Refrain

Jesus said: I am the life, far from whom no thing can grow,
but receive this living bread, and my Spirit you shall know.

Refrain

Prayer

O Living God, fill us with the presence of your Son, our Savior, Jesus
Christ, that we may know the joy of his presence as we partake of the
feast at his holy table. Amen.

Adam and Eve in the Garden of Eden by
Johann Wenzel Peter, c. 1800–1829

The Lord God created Adam and Eve and placed them
in the beautiful Garden of Eden. Adam tilled the ground
and kept it. His work was not a burden, but a delight.

No Work

The Lord God took the man and put him in the
Garden of Eden to till it and keep it.

Genesis 2:15

For centuries the Christian Church has baptized and confirmed its
members. I was baptized into the name of God the Father, Son, and
Holy Spirit at St. Lucas Slovak Evangelical Lutheran Church in St.
Louis, Missouri, in January 1952. It was the church my maternal
grandparents attended and my parents were married there.

Since I attended Emmaus Lutheran Elementary School, it was natural
for me to be confirmed with my classmates in that school when I was
in the eighth grade. So on Pentecost Sunday in 1965, I was confirmed
with about twenty other students at Emmaus Lutheran Church,
which originated as a German Lutheran mission church in South
St. Louis.

Pastor Wilson prepared us for Confirmation Sunday, when we would
affirm our baptism with the Apostles' Creed. Confirmation would
also include the laying on of hands and praying for the Holy Spirit
to enter our lives. But as was the practice in this congregation and in
other Lutheran congregations, Confirmation Sunday was preceded
by Examination Sunday.

Examination Sunday brought with it a bit of fear and apprehension for me and other confirmands. That was the Sunday when Pastor Wilson asked us questions about our Christian faith. It was a part of the Sunday service where we could shine by giving quick and intelligent answers about Bible stories, Martin Luther's Small Catechism, and the meaning of the Christian life. We also realized that incorrect and strange answers made us look foolish and uninformed in front of the entire congregation.

As it turned out I should have studied a lot more before Examination Sunday. On that Saturday night before the big day when I would sit with my classmates in front of a couple hundred people in the pews to answer questions about the Christian faith, I chose not to study or review the catechism or key stories of the Bible. Instead I did what any normal eighth-grade boy would do who loved sports. On that Saturday night, I played Wiffle ball with friends until dark. That proved to be my downfall and led to an embarrassing moment for me on Sunday morning.

So there I was with my classmates sitting in the choir loft on the left side of the church right next to the lectern. We were in good view of the congregation. They could clearly see us, and we could see them. Not one of us could hide on that Examination Sunday. I was all dressed up with a nice white shirt and clip-on tie. Like the other confirmation students, I wore a white robe, which looked like a choir gown.

The examination part of the service began. Pastor Wilson asked questions, and we responded as best as we could. Would this be a shining moment in my church life? Would this be a time for me to impress my parents, relatives, and the entire assembled congregation as I spoke the correct answers to several of Pastor Wilson's questions?

I wanted to choose the right moment to answer the theological questions. I decided to raise my hand to answer only the questions I was certain I knew. So when Pastor Wilson asked what it was like for Adam and Eve to live in the Garden of Eden, my hand shot up in the air like a rocket. I was certain I knew the answer to that question. I remembered the stories about Adam and Eve in the book of Genesis. I thought this was an easy question to answer. No sweat. I could not make a mistake answering this one.

I replied to Pastor Wilson's question about what it was like for Adam and Eve in the Garden of Eden with the words, "They didn't have to work." And then I saw a really confused and disappointed look on Pastor Wilson's face.

I was wrong. I gave the incorrect and shallow answer. Certainly Adam and Eve worked in the Garden of Eden, but their work was not a burden to them. Life was perfect for them until the Fall when they overstepped the boundaries God set for them and disobeyed him. Sin was nowhere in sight when God created them and put them in this beautiful paradise. But all of this faithful, peaceful, and joyful life came crashing down when Adam and Eve fell prey to the deceptive words of the serpent. They sinned when they ate the fruit from the tree God forbade them to touch. The consequences of their sin would not only corrupt them, but it would have fatal effects for humanity and all of God's creation. Sin and death would have its way and plague humanity. Eve would feel more pain in childbirth, and Adam would be burdened with work.

In my eighth-grade mind, perfection in the Garden of Eden for Adam and Eve meant no work at all. I guess I thought that play and good times were at the heart of life in paradise. So when I gave that answer to Pastor Wilson, he must have been taken aback at what I said. He never taught us about a work-free life in the Garden, but that was my definition of bliss in the eighth grade.

Nonetheless, Pastor Wilson still confirmed me the next Sunday. I am glad he did. After I affirmed my baptismal faith with the Apostles' Creed with my classmates, Pastor Wilson prayed for the Holy Spirit to be stirred up in my life. I needed that. I needed the Spirit to keep me faithful to Christ throughout my entire life and to help me understand the true meaning of Scripture.

In fact, I still recall my confirmation Bible verse from the second chapter of the book of Revelation: "Be faithful until death, and I will give you a crown of life."

Quotation from Martin Luther

Although individual Christians are thereby free from all works, they should nevertheless once again "humble themselves" in this freedom, take on "the form of a servant," "be made in human form and found in human vesture," and serve, help, and do everything for their neighbor, just as they see God has done and does with them through Christ.

Reflection

Have you experienced moments of freedom when you worked and served others for the sake of Christ? Can you recall a time when you realized that your work was no longer a delight but was a burden? How did you resolve your dilemma? Reflect upon the goodness of your work or vocation.

Hymn: "Hark, the Voice of Jesus Crying"

> Hark, the voice of Jesus crying,
> "Who will go and work today?
> Fields are white and harvests waiting—

Who will bear the sheaves away?"
Loud and long the Master calleth;
Rich reward He offers thee.
Who will answer, gladly saying,
"Here am I, send me, send me"?

If you cannot speak like angels,
If you cannot preach like Paul,
You can tell the love of Jesus,
You can say He died for all.
If you cannot rouse the wicked
With the judgment's dread alarms,
You can lead the little children
To the Savior's waiting arms.

Let none hear you idly saying,
"There is nothing I can do,"
While the multitudes are dying
And the Master calls for you.
Take the task He gives you gladly,
Let His work your pleasure be;
Answer quickly when He calleth,
"Here am I, send me, send me!"

Prayer

O Jesus, you call us to work in your kingdom. Give us the strength
to love our neighbors and to proclaim your promise of love. May our
hearts always be thankful for calling us to do your will in a world that
desperately needs your guidance and grace. Amen.

The Vision of Ezekiel by Francisco Collantes, 1630

The Lord God gave the prophet Ezekiel a vision of
hope with the valley of dry bones. The vision was
a promise to free the Israelites from captivity, as
well as a sign of the resurrection to come.

Mom's Vision

> The hand of the Lord came upon me, and he brought
> me out by the spirit of the Lord and set me down in
> the middle of a valley; it was full of bones.
>
> Ezekiel 37:1

My mother was a devout Christian. She always encouraged me to pray and made certain that the faith I received at my baptism was nurtured as I grew up. She and my father were insightful as they sent me to Lutheran schools where my Christian faith was nurtured and challenged. That Christian education experience, along with my attendance at Sunday school and Sunday worship, provided a solid foundation for the spiritual growth of my faith. As I reflect upon those developing years, I realize that it was a catalyst for my future calling to be a parish pastor.

Now, I knew my mother's faith was strong. She told me that as a child her parents, who emigrated from Czechoslovakia to the United States, sent her to a Lutheran elementary school and made her attend confirmation classes at their church, which had a Slovak heritage. In fact, my mother took confirmation classes taught in the Slovak language. She said her father was especially pleased that she was bilingual and could excel in the Slovak Lutheran confirmation class.

But besides that formal training in the Christian faith during her childhood, my mother also had a spiritual experience that she kept mostly to herself. She rarely talked about it at home and never shared the details of that spiritual moment with her close friends.

"When I was a child, I had a vision of Jesus," she told me. "I looked up into the sky and saw Jesus."

"Do you mean you saw clouds in the sky that looked like a picture of Jesus?" I asked.

"No," she answered, "I just saw Jesus as I looked up. I don't tell people about that because they wouldn't believe me."

But I believed my mother. I believed she had some kind of spiritual experience that deeply affected her life. I believed she had a vision that enriched her faith and assured her that her Lord was present in her life. Not many people can say that. In this postmodern age, visions are not easily believed. They are quickly discounted as a delusion or something caused by the side effect of a powerful drug.

My mother's strong faith in Christ was evident in her life. She was selfless. She always tried to please others. Her love was demonstrated to me many times. When I was three years old, the Salk vaccine was not yet on the market. I contracted a mild case of polio in one of my knees. My mother never gave up on me or gave in to this disease. She did as the doctor ordered. She exercised my knee daily, and in time the polio was gone. What determination she had to help with the healing process!

When her sister and brother-in-law opened up the first cafeteria-style steak restaurant in downtown St. Louis, my mother worked tirelessly to help this new business venture become successful. She managed the restaurant in the afternoons and early evenings. At the end of the day, she counted the cash receipts and made the night deposit at the bank. She loved her work to make that restaurant, which sold a steak dinner for $1.09 back in the early 1960s, become profitable and successful.

When one of her aunts was almost ninety years old, my mother invited her aunt to live with her and my father. My mother looked after her aunt's personal needs in her own home. It kept her aunt, a widow for many years, from having to spend all the money she had in the bank to live in an assisted living facility.

That vision of Jesus up in the heavens so inspired my mother that she led a life of faith and love. That vision was real to her. It was a sign of a living Lord who loved her and inspired her to share love on this earth with people the Holy Spirit sent her way.

Back in the sixth century BC, the prophet Ezekiel gave God the credit for the vision of dry bones that we read about in Ezekiel chapter 37. He wrote that the "hand of the Lord came upon me." That divine hand set this prophet down in the middle of a valley with dry bones scattered about. It seemed that this vision at first may have turned out to be a nightmare. Who wants to be surrounded with signs of death? Who wants to be enclosed in a dry valley with no signs of fresh, flowing water? Would God's vision to Ezekiel be one of doom and condemnation?

But Ezekiel's God was a God of mercy and hope. As the vision continued, God instructed Ezekiel to prophesy life to the dead, dry bones. The Lord said to this prophet, "Prophesy to these bones, and say to them: O dry bones, hear the word of the Lord. Thus says the Lord God to these bones: I will cause breath to enter you, and you shall live." (37:4–5)

As God breathed life into Adam at the beginning of creation, so God breathed again to give life. This time God's breath transformed dead bones and made them alive again. God's breath caused flesh to cover the bones, and this new life for God's people was filled with joy and thanksgiving.

Ezekiel's vision was good news for God's people, Israel, who struggled in Babylonian captivity. Israel longed for God to once again act on their behalf to rescue them as he had done long ago when they were in slavery in Egypt. Israel was like the dead, dry bones in the valley. Israel was lifeless and hopeless while in captivity in a foreign land.

Nonetheless, this vision of bones transformed into living, breathing human beings provided hope for God's chosen people. God freed them and led them back to the land promised to them through their ancestors. In this vision the Lord God said, "I am going to open your graves, and bring you up from your graves, O my people; and I will bring you back to the land of Israel. And you shall know that I am the Lord, when I open your graves, and bring you up from your graves, O my people. I will put my spirit within you, and you shall live, and I will place you on your own soil." (37:12–14)

Within a few decades the Lord worked through Cyrus of Persia to free his people once again. They returned to the land of promise and were strengthened to rebuild the Temple where the holy God dwelled.

As we reflect on this vision today, we see it as a divine promise of the resurrected life. The image of graves opened and the words "you shall live" point to the resurrected life offered to all who believe in God's Son, Jesus the Christ.

Visions are one way God communicates with his people. Certainly as my mother looked up into the sky and saw Jesus, it was an inspiring way God communicated with her when she was a child. The crucified and risen Lord Jesus Christ was constantly by her side in her times of joy and sorrow. That risen Lord promised to give the resurrected life to my mother and to all who trust in his gracious promises.

Quotation from Martin Luther

The Holy Spirit must always work in us through the word, granting us daily forgiveness until we attain to that life where there will be no more forgiveness. In that life there will be only perfectly pure and holy people, full of integrity and righteousness, completely freed from sin, death, and all misfortune, living in new, immortal, and glorified bodies.

Reflection

We read of visions or dreams in the Bible as a way God communicated to his people. Joseph, Ezekiel, and Peter all had dreams or visions or were in a trance given by the Lord God with a divine message. Do you believe that God can still communicate with us by a dream? Have you or a friend had a dream with a divine message? Ezekiel's dream pointed to the resurrected life. What do you believe the resurrected life will be like? Do you agree with Martin Luther's description of it in the quotation above from his *Large Catechism*?

Hymn: "Be Thou My Vision"

Be thou my vision, O Lord of my heart;
naught be all else to me, save that thou art:
thou my best thought both by day and by night,
waking or sleeping, thy presence my light.

Be thou my wisdom, and thou my true word;
I ever with thee and thou with me, Lord.
Thou my soul's shelter, and thou my high tow'r,
raise thou me heav'nward, O Pow'r of my pow'r.

Riches I heed not, nor vain, empty praise,
thou mine inheritance, now and always;
thou and thou only, the first in my heart,
great God of heaven, my treasure thou art.

Light of my soul, after victory won,
may I reach heaven's joys, O heaven's Sun!
Heart of my own heart, whatever befall,
still be my vision, O Ruler of all.

Prayer

All praise and thanks be to thee, victorious Lord. You raise us up to new life in the midst of trouble. Give us a vision of your goodness and mercy that we may remain faithful to you. Amen.

Descent of the Holy Spirit upon the Apostles
by Joseph Vladimirov, 1666

On the day of Pentecost, the Holy Spirit appeared as tongues of
fire on the heads of the apostles, including Mary, the mother of
our Lord. In the image above, halos are substituted for tongues
of fire. Nonetheless, the gift of divine fire for the church was
a flame to ignite the bold, public witness of the apostles.

Fire in the Church

When the day of Pentecost had come, they were all together in one place. And suddenly from heaven there came a sound like the rush of a violent wind, and it filled the entire house where they were sitting. Divided tongues, as of fire, appeared among them, and a tongue rested on each of them.

Acts 2:1–3

When we think of fire in the church, our minds turn to the second chapter of the book of the Acts of the Apostles on the day of Pentecost. The Holy Spirit's presence inspired the apostles to speak in other languages and witness to the saving love of Jesus of Nazareth as the one God anointed to be the Messiah. The visible sign of the Holy Spirit's presence was tongues or flames of fire that rested upon the head of each apostle.

I always thought of fire in the church in that way—Pentecost—until one day there was a fire of another sort. It was not the fire of the Holy Spirit. It was the fire of destruction with flames, smoke, and soot. It was a fire that brought fear to my life.

One afternoon I had returned to my church after having lunch with fellow pastors. I sat comfortably in my office working on a sermon for Sunday when I was interrupted by what I thought was the rustling of paper falling down from one of the walls in the fellowship hall. At first,

I dismissed that sound, but then I heard it again. Was someone in the fellowship hall unbeknownst to me? Hadn't our church secretary and the teachers in our mother's day out ministry gone home for the day? I thought there was no one else in the building. I rose from my chair, walked to the entrance of the fellowship hall, and looked around to see what was going on.

Then I saw it. I saw the smoke billowing from kitchen supplies near the stove at the end of the fellowship hall. Smoke began to fill the room. I wasted no time and hurried back to my office to call the fire department. By that time, more and more smoke filled the air. I needed to leave that church building as quickly as I could, but I hesitated. I thought that I could not let that fire burn up all of my books and vestments. I had so much money invested in them. So instead of running out of the building and waiting for the firefighters to arrive, I ran to the closet in my office and gathered an armful of vestments—alb, cassock, stoles, cinctures, chasubles, and cope. At least I could save those clergy clothes.

I quickly took them outside away from the smoke-filled section of the building and put them safely in my car. I ran back to the church entrance thinking I could safely enter and gather more of my valuable belongings from my office. But I stopped. The smoke was much too dense to navigate safely to my office. I stepped back from the door a few paces and just stood on the parking lot feeling helpless and wondering how much damage the fire in the fellowship hall would cause.

In a few minutes, I heard the siren of the fire truck. It sped up the church's driveway. The firefighters quickly entered the church and extinguished the fire. The fire itself was contained to the fellowship hall, but soot spread throughout the church building through the ducts of the heating and air conditioning system. It made for a massive cleanup from a professional cleaning crew. I was relieved that no one was in the building except for me.

Fire in Scripture is associated with judgment on the last day. But thank God the story does not end there. Sometimes, fire is seen in a good light. John the Baptist proclaimed that Jesus the Messiah would baptize his followers with the Holy Spirit and fire. That fire pointed to the day of Pentecost where tongues or flames of fire rested on the head of each apostle so they could preach about God's saving love through the death and resurrection of the Lord Jesus Christ.

Peter's sermon on Pentecost stirred the hearts of all the Jews who listened to him. He preached that God made Jesus "Lord and Messiah." They were so moved by Peter's preaching that they asked the apostles what they should do to be saved. Peter replied that they should repent and be baptized for the forgiveness of sins and to receive the promised Holy Spirit. A mass baptism followed with three thousand Jews receiving God's grace through water and the word.

With the Holy Spirit in their lives, "They devoted themselves to the apostles' teaching and fellowship, to the breaking of bread and the prayers." (Acts 2:42) The church began as the fire of the Holy Spirit descended on the apostles and spread into the hearts of the Jews who committed themselves to following Jesus as Lord. With the fire of the Spirit, a new community, a second Israel, was formed, and the church of Jesus Christ would spread to the ends of the earth.

Quotation from Martin Luther

But God's Spirit alone is called a Holy Spirit, that is, the one who has made us holy and still makes us holy. As the First Person of the Trinity is called a Creator and the Son is called a Redeemer, so on account of her work the Holy Spirit must be called a Sanctifier, or one who makes us holy.

Reflection

Have you ever been in a fire? What was your reaction? Jesus sent the promised Holy Spirit to the apostles on the day of Pentecost. In Acts chapter 2, what was the result of the gift of the Holy Spirit for the Christian church? The fruits of the Holy Spirit in Galatians chapter 5 include "love, joy, peace, patience, kindness, gentleness and self-control." Think about how one or more of these fruits of the Spirit have been shown in your life.

Hymn: "Come, Gracious Spirit, Heavenly Dove"

Come, gracious Spirit, heav'nly dove,
with light and comfort from above.
Come, be our guardian and our guide;
o'er ev'ry thought and step preside.

The light of truth to us display
and make us know and choose your way;
plant holy fear in ev'ry heart,
that we from God may ne'er depart.

Lead us to Christ, the living way,
nor let us from his pastures stray.
Lead us in holiness, the road
that we must take to dwell with God.

Lead us to heav'n, that we may share
fullness of joy forever there;
lead us to our eternal rest,
to be with God forever blest.

Prayer

Come, Holy Spirit, Living Fire, and kindle in our hearts the flame of love. Enlighten our paths in this world so that we may proclaim your saving deeds among all nations. Amen.

Abraham Serving the Three Angels by Rembrandt van Rijn, 1646

Abraham and Sarai demonstrated the Israelite
custom of hospitality as they welcomed the
unexpected three angels to their home.

A Florida Welcome

> The Lord appeared to Abraham by the oaks of
> Mamre, as he sat at the entrance of his tent in the
> heat of the day. He looked up and saw three men
> standing near him. When he saw them, he ran from
> the tent entrance to meet them, and bowed down to
> the ground.
>
> Genesis 18:1–2

We usually keep our distance from strangers. We do not know what to expect from them. We tell our children not to talk to strangers and to turn down the invitation of a stranger. We find it very difficult to welcome strangers in our lives unless they come highly recommended from friends or family members.

My wife, Priscilla, and I were strangers when we attended a popular revival in Pensacola, Florida, which was held at the Brownsville Assembly of God Church. We had visited Pensacola before and had seen some of its tourist attractions, but we had never set foot in the Assembly of God church. It was an all-expenses paid trip given by a member of my congregation who thought we would benefit from the deeply inspirational gathering.

I never made it a practice to attend religious revivals, although I attended one when I was a child out of curiosity. That was not part of my Christian upbringing. Nonetheless, we drove from our home in Mobile to the church in Pensacola for a revival that was gaining popularity and that attracted Christians who had traveled many miles to attend that Spirit-filled event. (I remember that this congregation had been praying for a revival and began one on Father's Day in 1995. An article I read about the Brownsville Revival reported that four million people attended this six day a week revival from 1995 to 2000.)

As we drove onto the church parking lot, we were welcomed by a teenage boy and girl dressed in their Sunday best who directed us to our parking spot.

That was welcome number one.

As we exited our car, another teenager directed us to the registration tent. As we signed up and got our name tags, we were welcomed again with a smile by the woman sitting behind the registration table.

That was welcome number two.

We walked a little way to the doors of the church. Those doors were opened by ushers who greeted us warmly and welcomed us into the church gathering area.

That was welcome number three.

As we walked across that gathering area to the actual doors of the sanctuary, another set of ushers saw us coming. They, too, opened the doors for us and greeted us.

That was welcome number four.

Four times. Four times we were lovingly welcomed by the folks of the Brownsville Assembly of God Church even before we found a seat in the church's sanctuary.

Even though we were an hour early before starting time, the church was packed. No seats in the pews were available. We stood at the sanctuary doors for a moment. Then an usher told us to follow her to the very front of the church where folding chairs were being set up in neat rows for us and for the overflow crowd. That was another kind gesture that we deeply appreciated.

But after about an hour of sitting on a hard folding chair, I got up and walked to the gathering area to stretch my legs and relieve the tension on my lower back. In that gathering area I met a staff member who struck up a conversation with me and learned that I needed a softer seat to enjoy the first night of the revival.

She said, "Follow me. I have a seat for you." Without hesitation I followed her, but I was not sure where we were going. She led me down a side aisle of the sanctuary and up the steps of the stage where the choir was seated. There was an empty seat there. She invited me to sit in a very comfortable padded chair in the back row of the choir on stage.

I was shocked. I was not going to sing with the choir and yet I was welcomed to sit in the empty chair in the choir section. I looked out into the assembly and saw my wife still sitting on a folding chair very near the stage up front. I waved to her. I smiled. She saw where I was sitting. We both were surprised that I had such a comfortable seat of honor for the revival. We were amazed that even though we were strangers in this Assembly of God church, we were welcomed multiple times. We were made to feel comfortable so we could enjoy the first night of the revival.

There is a familiar story in Genesis chapter 18 where Abraham welcomed three strangers into his household. Those three strangers were really messengers or angels from God who revealed to Abraham and Sarah that God promised to give them a son to fulfill the divine promise that Abraham would be the father of nations.

In Deuteronomy 10:19 we read the command God gave through Moses to the Israelites about hospitality: "You shall also love the stranger, for you were strangers in the land of Egypt." Indeed in the land of Egypt, God's people suffered under slavery. They were strangers in a strange land. What a difference hospitality would have made for them! Hospitality or welcoming would have been the compassionate thing to do, but instead God's people were treated harshly while they were strangers under the reign of terror from Pharaoh.

In the parable Jesus told about judgment day in Matthew chapter 25, we learn about ethics of the Christian life. Jesus said, "Then the king will say to those at his right hand, 'Come, you that are blessed by my Father, inherit the kingdom prepared for you from the foundation of the world; for I was hungry and you gave me food, I was thirsty and you gave me something to drink, I was a stranger and you welcomed me . . .'" (25:34–35).

Thus, welcoming the stranger is at the heart of Christian ministry. Welcoming is an essential part of Christian ethics. Welcoming is what the Lord expects from his faithful people who will inherit the fullness of the heavenly kingdom on the day of Christ's return to earth.

Moreover, the book of Hebrews echoes the same ethic of hospitality that we read about in Deuteronomy and in Matthew's gospel. Hebrews 13:2 says, "Do not neglect to show hospitality to strangers, for by doing that some have entertained angels without knowing it."

The overwhelming welcoming and hospitality we received at the Brownsville Assembly of God Church made a lasting impression on us. It impacted my ministry for years, and I made sure that I welcomed all strangers into the life of my congregation as best as I could. I tried to show them love and kindness following in the way of our Lord Jesus Christ.

And as we welcome strangers into our midst, we may indeed be welcoming angels sent by the Lord himself. Who knows for sure?

Quotation from Martin Luther

(On fulfilling the fifth commandment, "You shall not kill.") Patience, meekness, kindness, peacefulness, mercy, and in every circumstance a tender and friendly heart, devoid of all hatred, anger, and bitterness toward any person, even our enemies.

Reflection

Remember a time when you welcomed a stranger into your home, church, or business. What were the results of that welcoming? When you search for a new church home, do you look for one that truly welcomes you? How easy or difficult is it to rid ourselves of hatred and anger when we seek to welcome someone with whom we have had a serious disagreement? How do we overcome those feelings so that our hearts are filled with kindness and mercy to welcome the stranger or someone with whom we have deep differences of opinion?

Hymn: "Blest Be the Tie That Binds"

Blest be the tie that binds
our hearts in Christian love;
the unity of heart and mind
is like to that above.

Before our Father's throne
we pour our ardent prayers;
our fears, our hopes, our aims are one,
our comforts and our cares.

We share our mutual woes,
our mutual burdens bear,
and often for each other flows
the sympathizing tear.

From sorrow, toil, and pain,
and sin we shall be free;
and perfect love and friendship reign
through all eternity.

Prayer

God of Abraham and Jesus, you knock at the door of our hearts and desire to dwell within us. By the Holy Spirit help us to welcome you into our lives so that you abide with us with your never-failing love. Help us to share that love with those we do not know and so welcome them into the fellowship of believers. Amen.

The Raising of Lazarus by Claes Corneliszoon Moeyaert, 1654

The death of a loved one always seems to come too soon. Mary and Martha grieved the death of their brother, Lazarus. Jesus came amid their grief and raised Lazarus from the dead.

A Death Too Soon

> When he had said this, he cried with a loud voice,
> "Lazarus, come out!" The dead man came out, his
> hands and feet bound with strips of cloth, and his
> face wrapped in a cloth. Jesus said to them, "Unbind
> him, and let him go."
>
> John 11:43–44

I was nineteen years old and a freshman at the University of Missouri.
In many ways I was still naive. I had not suffered much at all, and
certainly the sting of death had only caused grief once in my life when
my maternal grandmother died when I was a high school student.
But in that freshman year, I would experience the shock and grief of
death that shook the foundation of my life.

One January afternoon after classes were done for the day, I knocked
on the door of a friend (let's call him Rick) who lived across the hall
from me in the dormitory. Rick loved to play basketball, and so did
I. But there was a warning. He had a heart condition, so he was not
supposed to overexert himself when he played. I never knew the exact
nature of that condition. Nonetheless, I knew I had to be careful
to make sure Rick did not exert himself too much or he could face
serious consequences.

So that afternoon we went to the gym to shoot baskets and get some exercise. I felt that would not hurt Rick. That would not put his life in jeopardy. His heart could take that kind of light exercise.

After a few minutes of shooting hoops, a couple of students asked us to play a game with them. Now these two guys were not weaklings. They were well-built. They appeared to me to be athletes on scholarship. Rick and I did not turn down their invitation. I thought the game would be all right for him. I would make sure he took it easy when he played and not run too hard, jump too high, or strain himself in any way.

But I was wrong—dead wrong. After we played a game of basketball with these two guys, Rick and I sat down on the gym floor to rest. Everything seemed to be going fine. Rick played well. He had not gotten hurt. I felt relieved that he made it through that competition. But then he fell to the floor. He was unconscious.

Fear swept over me. I got up and ran to the gym office to have someone call an ambulance. In a few minutes the emergency medical team attended to Rick as he lay there on the gym floor. They quickly put him on a stretcher, carefully loaded him into the ambulance, and sped off to the university hospital.

It all happened so quickly. One minute Rick and I were having fun playing a game of basketball, but in the next minute what I hoped would never happen came to pass. Rick fainted. He was unconscious. Did he have a heart attack? Had he played too strenuously? Did I not take good care of him as I intended to do? So many thoughts and emotions shot through my mind.

What was I to do next? Fortunately, a perceptive and caring fellow student walked with me to the hospital on campus. We sat in the waiting room by the emergency entrance. We wondered what was happening to Rick. I do not remember the exact moment when I received word in the emergency waiting room that my friend died. Grief and shock set in, and I felt completely helpless. I blamed myself for his death. Oh, to turn back the clock! Oh, to never have invited him to shoot baskets! The sting of death of a college friend was a shock in itself, but to have been so closely associated with it was almost too much to bear.

I went back to my dorm room and shared the news with my roommate, who had been my friend since high school. He offered to call the campus Lutheran pastor for me. That would have been helpful, but I turned him down for some reason. Instead I talked to the residence hall assistant who was hired by the university to look after matters on my floor of the dormitory. I told him what happened.

Then I called my older cousin who was also a student at the university. He picked me up, and we drove to his house off campus. I spent the night there with him, and he offered me much needed support. He realized I was in shock. He cared about me. He was sensitive to what just happened in my life. He called my parents for me to let them know what had happened and the grief and shock I was experiencing.

It was not only shock and grief that shook me as a young man—it was also guilt. I felt guilty. I blamed myself for Rick's death. I thought I could care for him even though he had a bad heart and was not to overexert himself.

A couple of days later when I returned home to St. Louis, my father drove me to meet Rick's parents to explain to them what happened. I told his parents about the basketball game. Rick's father wanted to know if during the game, Rick was hit in the chest. I could not say for sure, but a blow to his chest may have caused his heart to fail and lead to his untimely death.

It seems that death always comes too soon no matter what age a person dies. During my ministry I presided at funerals for people of various ages, from a middle school boy who was struck by a car and suffered a tragic death to the elderly who led long and good lives and who died with dignity. In each case, death seemed to come too soon. Friends and relatives wished that their loved ones could live longer pain free, free from illness or strife, and enjoy the blessings God bestowed on them.

Jesus's good friend Lazarus died. Lazarus's sisters, Mary and Martha, were in grief along with all the citizens of the town of Bethany. When Jesus was still outside that village, Martha ran out to see her Lord. She was so disappointed that Jesus took too long to see her sick brother to heal him. She cried out to Jesus, "Lord, if you had been here, my brother would not have died." (John 11:21)

But Jesus assured Martha that Lazarus would live again. He said to her, "Your brother will rise again." (John 11:23) Martha believed Jesus's word and told him that her brother would come back to life at the time of the resurrection.

When Mary saw Jesus, she expressed the same sentiment as her sister, Martha. She repeated her sister's words, "Lord, if you had been here, my brother would not have died." (John 11:32)

Twice Jesus heard the cries of these sisters. Twice Jesus was reminded that he needed to drop what he was doing and attend to the important matter of healing a sick friend at the brink of death.

Receiving a double dose of grief from Mary and Martha, Jesus was deeply moved. He was disturbed. He wept. He went to Lazarus's tomb, which was a cave. The stone that sealed the tomb and marked the finality of death was rolled away at Jesus's request. Jesus prayed to his Father in heaven and then with a loud voice he cried out, "Lazarus, come out!" (John 11:43)

Lazarus emerged from his tomb still wrapped with a burial cloth. He lived again, breathed again, and was welcomed back into his family and community. With Jesus, there is healing. With Jesus, there is life. With Jesus, there is a resurrected life for all who believe in him.

I have never forgotten that day in the gym when my friend, Rick, suddenly lost his life. I have tried to put it out of my mind over the years. Every time I think about his death at a young age, I grieve. I am saddened and I wish that I had taken better care of him. But at the same time, I believe that Rick will live again even as Lazarus was raised from the dead. I believe Rick will rise again on the day of resurrection and I will see him alive with a new and strong heart.

Quotation from Martin Luther

Baptism, then, signifies two things—death and resurrection, that is, full and complete justification. When the minister immerses the child in the water it signifies death, and when he draws it forth again it signifies life. Thus Paul expounds it in Romans 6:4, "Therefore we have been buried with (Christ) by baptism into his death, so that just as Christ was raised from the dead by the glory of the Father, so we too might walk in newness of life."

Reflection

Reflect on the first time a death of a friend or loved one brought you much sadness, anger, and grief. How did you deal with those feelings? Do you agree with Martin Luther's explanation that baptism signifies death and resurrection? Have you ever thought that immersion into water signifies death and drawing the person out of water signifies life in Christ? Is this immersion into water and drawing out of water an insightful way to understand the meaning of Holy Baptism?

Hymn: "Thine Is the Glory"

Thine is the glory, risen, conqu'ring Son;
endless is the vict'ry thou o'er death hast won!
Angels in bright raiment rolled the stone away,
kept the folded grave clothes where thy body lay.
Thine is the glory, risen, conqu'ring Son;
endless is the vict'ry thou o'er death hast won!

Lo, Jesus meets thee, risen from the tomb!
Lovingly he greets thee, scatters fear and gloom;
let his church with gladness hymns of triumph sing,
for the Lord now liveth; death hath lost its sting!
Thine is the glory, risen, conqu'ring Son;
endless is the vict'ry thou o'er death hast won!

No more we doubt thee, glorious Prince of life;
life is naught without thee; aid us in our strife;
make us more than conqu'rors, through thy deathless love;
bring us safe through Jordan to thy home above.
Thine is the glory, risen, conqu'ring Son;
endless is the vict'ry thou o'er death hast won!

Prayer

Victorious Lord, as you raised Lazarus from the grave, so raise us up to new life as we daily repent of our sins and hold onto your promise of grace. Keep us faithful until the day of resurrection when we enjoy the fullness of salvation. Amen.

The Agony in the Garden of Gethsemane by
Raffaello Sanzio de Urbino (Raphael), 1504

In a few quiet moments before his betrayal, Jesus
prayed that the will of his heavenly Father be done.
When we pray, we open ourselves up to God like
Jesus and share our innermost thoughts.

PICC Line Prayer

And going a little farther, he threw himself on the ground and prayed, "My Father, if it is possible, let this cup pass from me; yet not what I want but what you want."

Matthew 26:39

I had emergency surgery to get rid of an internal infection near my left pelvis. When I had seen my orthopedic surgeon on a Monday afternoon for a checkup, she had broken the news to me that I needed immediate surgery. So I was admitted to the hospital that evening, and the next morning I was in the operating room with a team of surgeons performing surgery on my left pelvis.

During my almost weeklong stay in the hospital, I began to receive powerful antibiotics through a PICC line (peripherally inserted central catheter). This catheter was inserted through my upper arm and reached right next to my heart. It was a delicate procedure performed under sterile conditions in the hospital.

Each evening a well-educated nurse administered two drugs through that catheter. But receiving a few days of antibiotics by a PICC line was not nearly enough medicine to safeguard against the infection returning. My orthopedic surgeon and an infectious disease doctor wanted me to have six weeks of these antibiotics on a daily basis to make certain the infection was cleared up. That was medical protocol.

That order meant that my wife, Priscilla, would take over giving me the antibiotics for the next five weeks in our home.

So before we left the hospital, a nurse gave my wife a crash course on PICC line procedures. To make matters a bit easier, the nurse sent Priscilla home with a chart that clearly laid out the steps to administer the drugs through that central catheter. Priscilla had to "scrub the hub" of the PICC line, flush the PICC line with a saline solution, slowly give me one of the antibiotics through that catheter over a five-minute period, and finally attach a round-looking ball of antibiotics about the size of an orange to my PICC line. This last antibiotic took two hours to administer. So I sat at the kitchen table each night for almost five weeks reading a book or going online with my laptop to pass the time.

Now it is one thing to take a crash course in PICC line procedures and watch someone else do it at the hospital, but it is another thing to actually do this at home without a supervising nurse making sure all goes well with the step-by-step procedure. Even though my wife is very talented, she felt hesitant about giving me antibiotics through the PICC line at home. She wanted more training to feel confident with this procedure. So she prayed for help. She prayed for God to work out a way to help her give me the antibiotics in the proper and safe way.

As God would have it, two of our friends gave us a phone call when we arrived home. They were making their annual trip to their condominium in Florida from their home in St. Louis. That husband and wife always spent the night with us when they made their trip to the Sunshine State. The husband was a Lutheran pastor who had plenty of practice in pastoral care, and his wife had been a PICC line nurse for over ten years.

Priscilla's prayer was answered. God sent the help she needed and help for me, too, through our two friends. They stayed for two nights. The pastor provided spiritual support through prayer and holy conversations, and the nurse reviewed with Priscilla the procedures for giving me antibiotics through that central catheter.

Through their visit we believed that God heard our prayers and cared about us through our two longtime friends who traveled to their winter home in Florida. They even taught us a new card game that we played each night and took our minds off of the medical procedures to come for the next five weeks.

Just before Jesus was arrested, he went to the Garden of Gethsemane to pray. He took along with him the disciples Peter and the two sons of Zebedee. Jesus knew that his hour had come to give up his life through an ugly death on the cross. Nonetheless, trusting in his Father in heaven, Jesus prayed, "My Father, if it is possible, let this cup pass from me, yet not what I want but what you want." (Matthew 26:39)

Jesus could have escaped what was to come. He could have hidden during the night so that no one could find him. But instead he faced what was the Father's will for the salvation of the whole world. Jesus prayed for God's will to be done.

Earlier in the Gospel of St. Matthew, Jesus taught his disciples to pray, and one petition of the prayer said, "Your kingdom come. Your will be done, on earth as it is in heaven." (Matthew 6:10) Even in Jesus's last moments before his death, he prayed again, "Father, forgive them; for they do not know what they are doing." (Luke 23:34)

Prayer is an essential part of the Christian life. In prayer we open ourselves up to God. We express our needs and wants. We pray for others. We give God praise and thanksgiving for the multitude of gifts he graciously gives to us. St. Paul even encourages us to pray as much as we can. He wrote, "Pray in the Spirit at all times in every prayer and supplication." (Ephesians 6:18)

Priscilla's PICC line prayer was offered up to God. God heard what was on her heart and mind. And God granted her the help she needed to care for me through trusted friends.

Quotation from Martin Luther

It is a good thing to let prayer be the first business of the morning and the last at night. Diligently guard against those false, deluding ideas, which tell you, "Wait a little while. I will pray in an hour; first I must attend to this or that."

Reflection

Think about your spiritual practice for praying daily. Do you look for prayer resources in devotional books, online religious websites, and in your church's hymnal? Which of these resources have you found to be helpful for your faith and daily prayer time? Find an article online for the Liturgy of the Hours or Breviary and discern if this is a helpful practice for your daily life. Do you agree that prayer should be the first order of business for the day? What things detract you from moments of prayer? How can you cultivate a deeper spiritual life through prayer?

Hymn: "Lord, Teach Us How to Pray Aright"

Lord, teach us how to pray aright, with rev'rence and with fear.
Though dust and ashes in your sight, we may, we must draw near.

We perish if we cease from prayer; oh, grant us pow'r to pray.
And when to meet you we prepare, Lord, meet us on our way.

Give deep humility; the sense of godly sorrow give;
a strong desire, with confidence, to hear your voice and live;

Faith in the only sacrifice that can for sin atone;
to cast our hopes, to fix our eyes on Christ, on Christ alone.

Give these, and then your will be done;
thus strengthened with all might,
we, through your Spirit and your Son, shall pray, and pray aright.

Prayer

Eternal God, Father, Son, and Holy Spirit, may our prayers rise to you as incense and may your will be done on this earth as it is in heaven. Amen.

Christ and the Samaritan Woman at the Well
by Jacob van Oost the Younger, 1668

As Jesus and his disciple stopped to rest at Jacob's
well, Jesus started a holy conversation with a
Samaritan woman. He offered her living water to call
her to faith and to the promise of eternal life.

Living Water

Jesus said to her, "Everyone who drinks of this water
will be thirsty again, but those who drink of the
water that I will give them will never be thirsty. The
water that I will give will become in them a spring
of water gushing up to eternal life."

John 4:13–14

Making the sign of the cross upon one's self was something only
Catholics practiced during Mass. That was something I learned when
I was a child because my many Catholic friends practiced that ritual.
As a Lutheran back in the 1950s, I would never do anything like
that. That was something I thought was reserved for Catholics. It
seemed mysterious to me to make the sign of the cross. I did not
know what religious significance it held for the Catholics who did
this each Sunday.

But times have changed. The ecumenical movement has drawn
Catholics and Lutherans closer together in a series of official
dialogues for the past several decades. When the publishing company
of the Lutheran Church in America, Fortress Press, came out with
a new worship book in the late 1970s, it included rubrics on how to
worship. One of those permissive rubrics was to make the sign of the
cross to remember one's baptism into Christ. So now Lutherans were
encouraged to do something Catholics had done for years—make the
sign of the cross during worship.

I thought that this liturgical practice was something that could become meaningful to the members of my congregation I served during my active ministry. But how was I to encourage this practice? How was I to encourage members of my congregation to dip a finger into the water of the baptismal font and make the sign of the cross on their forehead to remember their own baptism and its importance?

I started with children's sermon. Early on in my ministry I included children's sermons in Sunday worship. I tried to make one simple point about the love of Christ as I talked to them for a moment or two. Sometimes I used objects to make that point, such as a cross to remember Jesus's death on the cross or a paper crown that I got from a fast food burger restaurant to remind children that Jesus is the good king who loves and protects them.

For my children's sermons I invited the children to leave their seats in the pews and meet me at the baptismal font. I then asked them to dip a finger into the water and make the sign of the cross on their foreheads. I encouraged them to say, "I am baptized. Jesus loves me. I will follow Jesus."

I thought that this might be a way to help them remember that they are children of God. They are in God's family. I also hoped that when adults in the congregation saw that happening week after week in the worship service that they, too, would follow in the same manner. When they entered the nave, they could walk to the font, dip their finger in the bowl of water, make the sign of the holy cross on their forehead, and remember their baptism in the name of God the Father, Son, and Holy Spirit. And in that spiritually refreshing moment, contemplate the gift of living water from the Christ who drenches us from head to toe with his grace.

A discussion about water flows throughout the story of Jesus and the Samaritan woman at Jacob's well.

Jesus and his disciples were traveling from Judea to Galilee by way of Samaria. They stopped in the city of Sychar to rest and to gain strength by eating and drinking. But where would they find water to quench their thirst? At noon they came to the place called Jacob's well. It was there that Jesus had a conversation with a Samaritan woman about water.

Breaking a long-standing tradition of not speaking to people of Samaria, Jesus, a Jew, asked for a drink of water from the Samaritan woman. She had come to the well at noon to draw water. Shocked that Jesus would even speak to her, she wanted to know the reason he broke down the wall of separation and wanted that drink of water from her. Jesus said that if she knew the gift of God and who was asking for a drink, she would have asked him for living water. At that point the Samaritan woman did not know Jesus was the long hoped for Messiah who could give God's gift of living water.

Intrigued by Jesus's comment, she continued the conversation and asked, "Sir, you have no bucket, and the well is deep. Where do you get that living water?" (John 4:11) Her focus was on the water in the well. She thought Jesus was referring to the earthly element at the bottom of the well, which was life-saving for all who drank from it.

But Jesus spoke metaphorically about that living water. He said to her, "Everyone who drinks of this water will be thirsty again, but those who drink of the water that I will give them will never be thirsty. The water that I will give will become in them a spring of water gushing up to eternal life." (John 4:13–14) Excited and amazed at what Jesus offered, she immediately replied, "Sir, give me this water, so that I may never be thirsty or have to keep coming here to draw water." (4:15)

As this story continued, the Samaritan woman recognized Jesus as a prophet because he somehow knew her background of having several husbands. Before she left the well and returned home to the city, Jesus revealed to her that he was the Messiah. That news was too good to keep to herself. Was Jesus, the Jewish man who asked her for a drink at Jacob's well, really the anointed one God sent to save his people? The woman finally believed in him, and that transforming moment inspired her to say to the people of Sychar, "Come and see a man who told me everything I have ever done! He cannot be the Messiah, can he?" (John 4:29)

The woman at the well tasted the living water Jesus offered. That living water was not something she earned. It was a gift. It was the knowledge that Jesus himself was the Messiah and the faith to believe in him as the one sent from God to save her and others from their sins.

Living water is God's grace freely and abundantly given to us through Jesus Christ. Through his suffering, death, and resurrection, Jesus gives us the water of life to make our troubled souls well again.

Throughout the Gospel of John, Jesus spoke metaphorically about himself just as he used the metaphor of living water with the Samaritan woman at the well. Jesus described himself through a series of "I am" statements in the Gospel of John:

"I am the bread of life." Jesus feeds and satisfies our hungry souls. (6:35)

"I am the light of the world." Jesus illuminates our lives so that we make decisions that are loving and caring and we walk in his ways. (8:12)

"I am the gate." Through Jesus we enter into the divine promise of eternal life. (10:7)

"I am the good shepherd." Jesus protects us when the troubles of this life threaten to overtake us and sling us into despair. (10:11)

"I am the resurrection and the life." All who have faith in Jesus have the promise of life eternal, which begins now and is brought to perfection in the life to come. (11:25)

"I am the way, and the truth, and the life." Following Jesus and hearing his word, we hold onto divine and timeless truths bringing us life in his name. (14:6)

"I am the vine." Connected to Jesus with a deep trust and confidence in him, we as his branches draw the sweetness of an abundant life. (15:5)

Living water was a gift to the woman at the well from Jesus, the Messiah. For us, living water that flows as a gift from the Lord Jesus Christ comes to us first in Holy Baptism. The living water of this sacrament is connected to Jesus's word and promise of life and salvation. We read in Mark 16:16, "The one who believes and is baptized will be saved."

That living water first given at baptism has daily ongoing significance for our lives. With the living water of Christ's mercy and grace, we can daily repent of our sins, hold onto Christ's promise of forgiveness, and be raised up to newness of life.

As baptized Christians we joyfully remember Christ's promise of life and salvation as we dip our finger into the baptismal bowl of water and make the sign of the cross on our foreheads.

Quotation from Martin Luther

What is baptism? Namely, that it is not simply plain water, but water placed in the setting of God's word and commandment and made holy by them. It is nothing else than God's water, not that the water itself is nobler than other water but that God's word and command are added to it.

Reflection

Remember the faith moments in your life when you received living water as a gift from the crucified, risen, and ascended Jesus Christ. Reflect on those moments. How do we celebrate and give thanks for those spiritually refreshing moments in our lives?

Hymn: "All Who Believe and Are Baptized"

All who believe and are baptized
shall see the Lord's salvation;
baptized into the death of Christ,
they are a new creation;
through Christ's redemption they will stand
among the glorious heav'nly band
of ev'ry tribe and nation.

With one accord, O God, we pray,
grant us your Holy Spirit;
help us in our infirmity
through Jesus' blood and merit;
grant us to grow in grace each day
by holy baptism, that we may
eternal life inherit.

Prayer

Gracious, blessed Trinity, Father, Son, and Holy Spirit, we give you thanks and praise for the gift of living water that refreshes our souls and makes us whole in your holy name. Amen.

The peace of the Lord be with you always.

+ + +

Acknowledgments

I dedicate this book to my children, Katie and Michael, their spouses Neal and Liz respectively, and to my grandchildren, Grace and Olivia. Their love and support truly uplifts my spirit.

I am grateful for the editorial services of Carolina VonKampen (carolinavonkampen.com). Her careful review of my book provided the editorial boost it needed to make my devotions more compelling to readers.

Notes

Front Cover

Angelika Kauffmann, *Christus und die Samaritern am Brunnen*, 1796, oil on canvas, 123.5 cm × 158.5 cm, Neue Pinakothek, Munich, accessed through Wikipedia Commons. Public domain.

God's Tattoo

Rembrandt van Rijn, *The Baptism of the Eunuch*, 1626, oil on oak panel, 64 cm × 47.5 cm, Museum Catharijneconvent, Utrecht, accessed through Wikipedia Commons. Public domain.

Martin Luther, "The Holy and Blessed Sacrament of Baptism, 1519," in *The Annotated Luther* Vol. 1, *The Roots of Reform*, ed. Timothy J. Wengert (Minneapolis: Fortress Press, 2015), 208. Used by permission.

Thomas H. Kingo, "On My Heart Imprint Your Image," in *Evangelical Lutheran Worship Pew Edition* (Minneapolis: Augsburg Fortress, 2006), 811. Public domain.

Water Rescue

Marten Pepijn, *Crossing of the Red Sea*, 1626, oil on panel, 169 cm × 242 cm, Royal Museum of Fine Arts Antwerp, Antwerp, accessed through Wikipedia Commons. Public domain.

Martin Luther, "The Holy and Blessed Sacrament of Baptism, 1519," in *The Annotated Luther* Vol. 1, *The Roots of Reform*, ed. Timothy J. Wengert (Minneapolis: Fortress Press, 2015), 208. Used by permission.

Benjamin Schmolck, "Dearest Jesus, We Are Here," trans. Catherine Winkworth, in *Evangelical Lutheran Worship Pew Edition* (Minneapolis: Augsburg Fortress, 2006), 443. Public domain.

Revival Time

El Greco, *Pentecost*, c. 1600, oil on canvas, 275 cm × 127 cm, Museo del Prado, Madrid, accessed through Wikipedia Commons. Public domain.

Martin Luther, *The Large Catechism of Dr. Martin Luther, 1529: The Annotated Luther Study Edition*, ed. Kirsi I. Stjerna (Minneapolis: Fortress Press, 2016), 358–9. Used by permission.

Martin Luther and traditional German hymn text, "Come, Holy Ghost, God and Lord," trans. composite, in *Evangelical Lutheran Worship Pew Edition* (Minneapolis: Augsburg Fortress, 2006), 395. Public domain.

My Communion

Hans Holbein the Younger, *The Last Supper*, c. 1524–1525, oil on limewood panel, 115.5 cm × 97.3 cm, Kunstmuseum, Basel, accessed through Wikipedia Commons. Public domain.

Martin Luther, "The Blessed Sacrament of the Holy and True Body of Christ, and the Brotherhoods, 1519," in *The Annotated Luther*

Vol. 1, *The Roots of Reform*, ed. Timothy J. Wengert (Minneapolis: Fortress Press, 2015), 233. Used by permission.

Anonymous, "I Received the Living God," in *Evangelical Lutheran Worship Pew Edition* (Minneapolis: Augsburg Fortress, 2006), 477. Public domain.

No Work

Johann Wenzel Peter, *Adam and Eve in the Garden of Eden*, c. 1800–1829, oil on canvas, 247 cm × 336 cm, Vatican Pinacoteca, Vatican City, accessed through Wikipedia Commons. Public domain.

Martin Luther, "The Freedom of a Christian, 1520," in *The Annotated Luther* Vol. 1, *The Roots of Reform*, ed. Timothy J. Wengert (Minneapolis: Fortress Press, 2015), 522–3. Used by permission.

Daniel March, "Hark, the Voice of Jesus Crying," stanzas 1, 2, and 4, in *Lutheran Service Book* (St. Louis: Concordia Publishing House, 2006), 826. Public domain.

Mom's Vision

Francisco Collantes, *The Vision of Ezekiel*, 1630, oil on canvas, 177 cm × 205 cm, Museo del Prado, Madrid, accessed through Wikipedia Commons. Public domain.

Martin Luther, *The Large Catechism of Dr. Martin Luther, 1529: The Annotated Luther Study Edition*, ed. Kirsi I. Stjerna (Minneapolis: Fortress Press, 2016), 363–4. Used by permission.

Traditional Irish hymn text, "Be Thou My Vision," vers. Eleanor H. Hull, trans. Mary E. Byrne, in *Evangelical Lutheran Worship Pew Edition* (Minneapolis: Augsburg Fortress, 2006), 793. Public domain.

Fire in the Church

Joseph Vladimirov, *Descent of the Holy Spirit upon the Apostles*, 1666, 105 cm × 62 cm, Trinity Church in Nikitniki, Moscow, accessed through Wikipedia Commons. Public domain.

Martin Luther, *The Large Catechism of Dr. Martin Luther, 1529: The Annotated Catechism of Dr. Martin Luther 1529*, ed. Kirsi I. Stjerna (Minneapolis: Fortress Press, 2016), 358–9. Used by permission.

Simon Brown, "Come, Gracious Spirit, Heavenly Dove," in *Evangelical Lutheran Worship Pew Edition* (Minneapolis: Augsburg Fortress, 2006), 404. Public domain.

A Florida Welcome

Rembrandt van Rijn, *Abraham Serving the Three Angels*, 1646, oil on panel, 16 cm × 21 cm, Aurora Trust, New York, accessed through Wikipedia Commons. Public domain.

Martin Luther, *Little Prayer Book, 1522 and A Simple Way to Pray, 1535: The Annotated Luther Study Edition*, ed. Mary Jane Haemig and Eric Lund (Minneapolis: Fortress Press, 2017), 176–7. Used by permission.

John Fawcett, "Blest Be the Tie That Binds," in *Evangelical Lutheran Worship Pew Edition* (Minneapolis: Augsburg Fortress, 2006), 656. Public domain.

A Death Too Soon

Claes Corneliszoon Moeyaert, *The Raising of Lazarus*, 1654, oil on oak, 83 cm × 118 cm, National Museum in Warsaw, Warsaw, accessed through Wikipedia Commons. Public domain.

Martin Luther, "The Babylonian Captivity of the Church, 1520," in *The Annotated Luther* Vol. 3, *Church and Sacraments*, ed. Paul W. Robinson (Minneapolis: Fortress Press, 2016), 70. Used by permission.

Edmond Budry, "Thine Is the Glory," trans. R. Birch Hoyle, in *Evangelical Lutheran Worship Pew Edition* (Minneapolis: Augsburg Fortress, 2006), 376. Public domain.

PICC Line Prayer

Raffaello (Raphael) Sanzio da Urbino, *The Agony in the Garden of Gethsemane*, 1504, oil on panel, 24.1 cm × 28.8 cm, Metropolitan Museum of Art, New York City, accessed through Wikipedia Commons. Public domain.

Martin Luther, *Little Prayer Book, 1522 and A Simple Way to Pray, 1535: The Annotated Luther Study Edition*, ed. Mary Jane Haemig and Eric Lund (Minneapolis: Fortress Press, 2017), 257. Used by permission.

James Montgomery, "Lord, Teach Us How to Pray Aright," in *Evangelical Lutheran Worship Pew Edition* (Minneapolis: Augsburg Fortress, 2006), 745. Public domain.

Living Water

Jacob van Oost the Younger, *Christ and the Samaritan Woman at the Well*, 1668, oil on canvas, 129.3 cm × 235.6 cm, private collection, accessed through Wikipedia Commons. Public domain.

Martin Luther, *The Large Catechism of Dr. Martin Luther 1529: The Annotated Luther Study Edition*, ed. Kirsi I. Stjerna (Minneapolis: Fortress Press, 2016), 391. Used by permission.

Thomas H. Kingo, "All Who Believe and Are Baptized," trans. George T. Rygh, in *Evangelical Lutheran Worship Pew Edition* (Minneapolis: Augsburg Fortress, 2006), 442. Public domain.

About the Author

Rev. Gary M. Schimmer was born and reared in St. Louis, Missouri. He was ordained in the Lutheran Church in America in 1978 and served congregations in Georgia, Alabama, Missouri, and Tennessee. He and his wife are retired and live in Nashville, Tennessee. They have two children and two grandchildren.

Rev. Schimmer has a bachelor of arts degree from the University of Missouri and a master of divinity degree from Vanderbilt Divinity School. He also studied Christian spirituality at Spring Hill College.

Printed in the United States
By Bookmasters